Kaleidoscope

A Meditative Colouring Book

By Kelly Foxton

ISBN 978-0-9919131-3-8

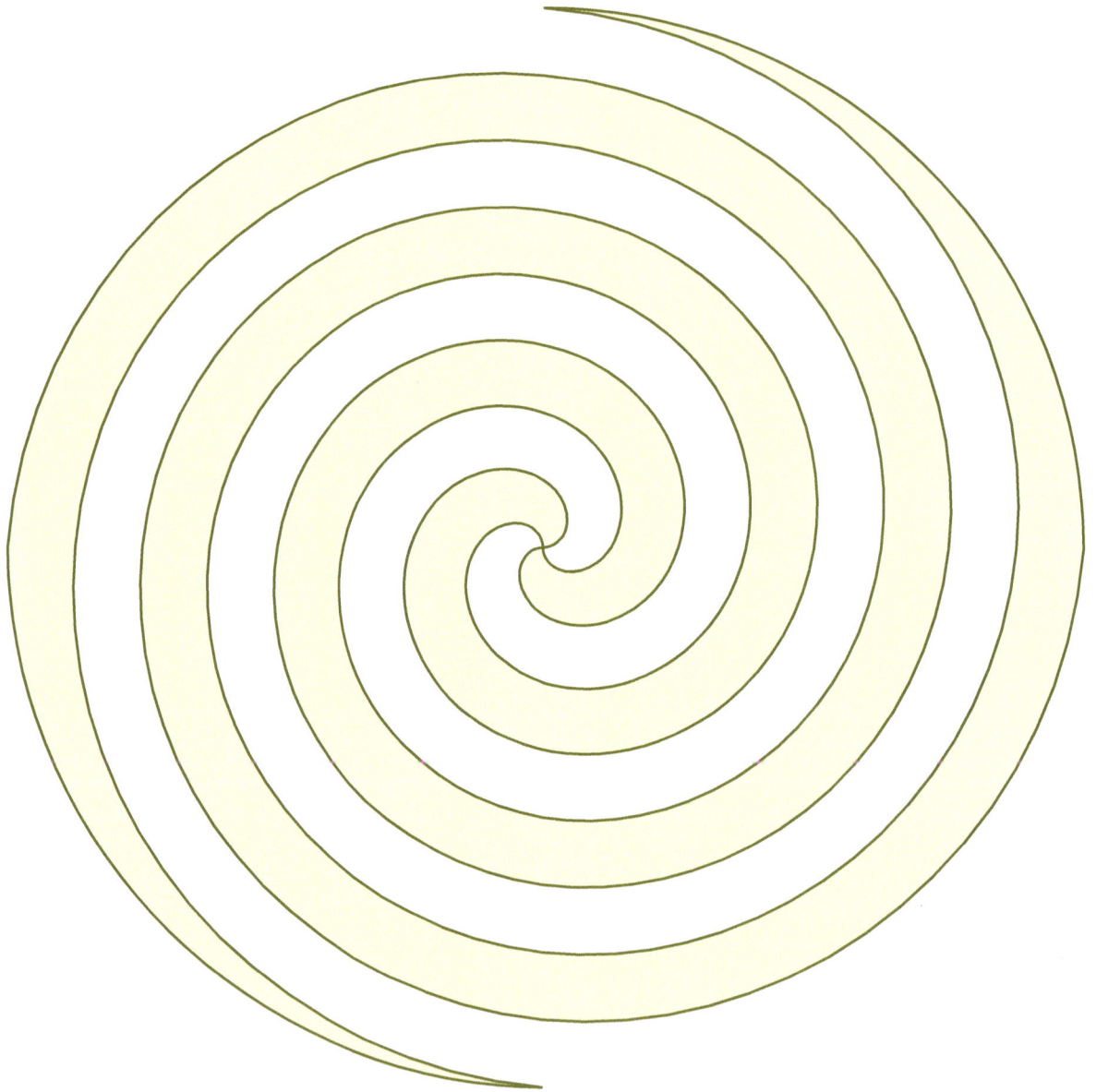

Welcome to my Kaleidoscoped World!

Every image on the following pages is a kaleidoscoped view of one of my original works of art. Even though very few bear any resemblance to the original piece, somehow these images managed to capture the essence and energy of their "parent" paintings in ways that surprised and delighted me.

I've tried to arrange the colouring pages according to their degree of intricacy. Images with bolder, simpler lines have been placed at the front of the book. Images with intricate detail and very thin outlines are arranged closer to the back.

I suggest you use coloured pencil as your medium in order to avoid any risk of liquid mediums, like marker or paint, soaking through and leaving stains or damp buckles in your paper. Be sure to have a good pencil sharpener on hand before you start as the detail in the more intricate images is quite fine.

Playing with, meditating with, reworking and spending countless hours with these images and their many incarnations has been a joy-filled experience for me. May the colours in your heart flow onto these pages as you make these images your own.

Wishing you peace, relaxation and above all, JOY!

Many blessings,

Kelly

Haven't coloured in a while? Don't worry, most of us haven't!

Here are a couple of warm-up pages to get you started...

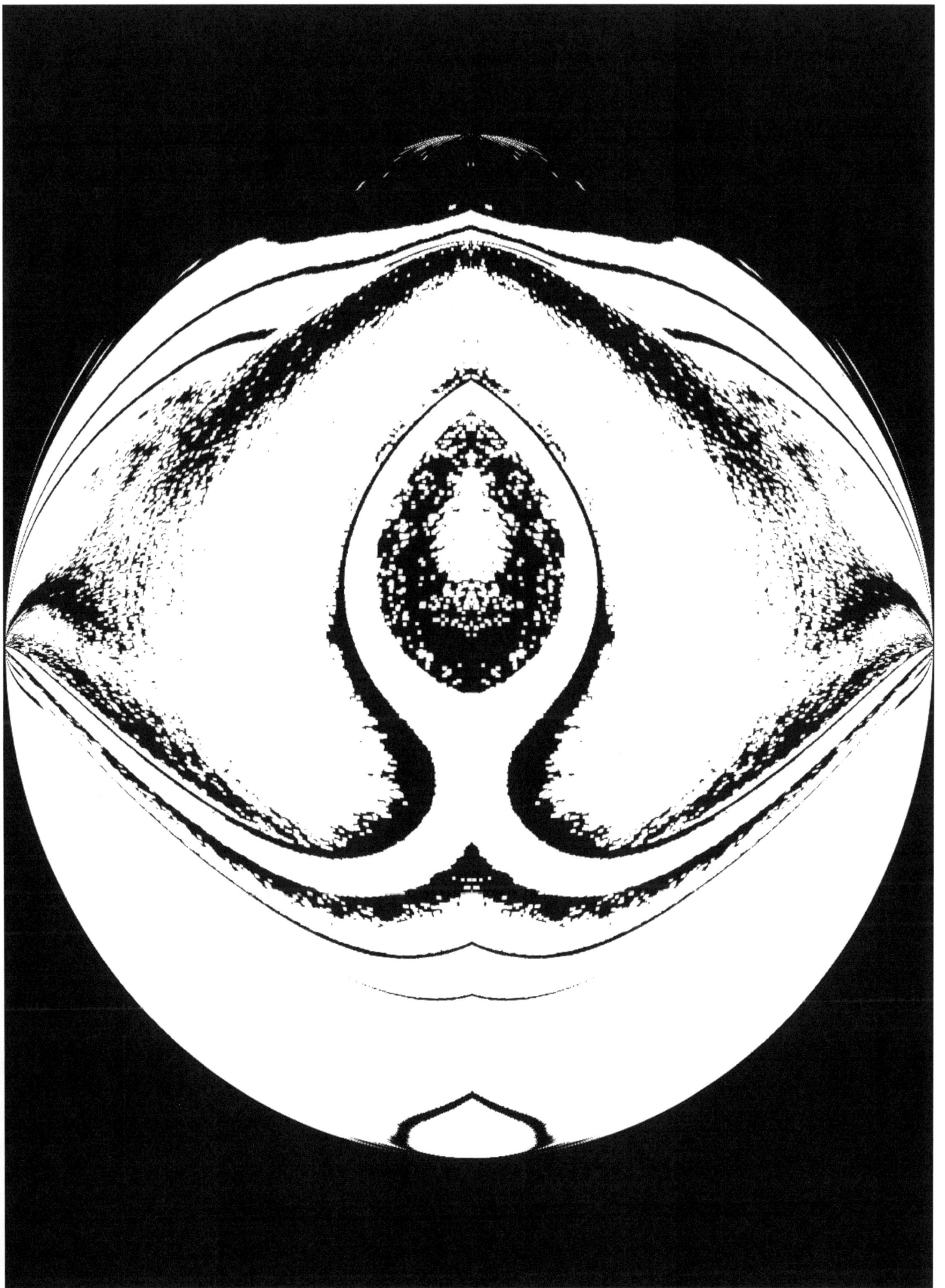

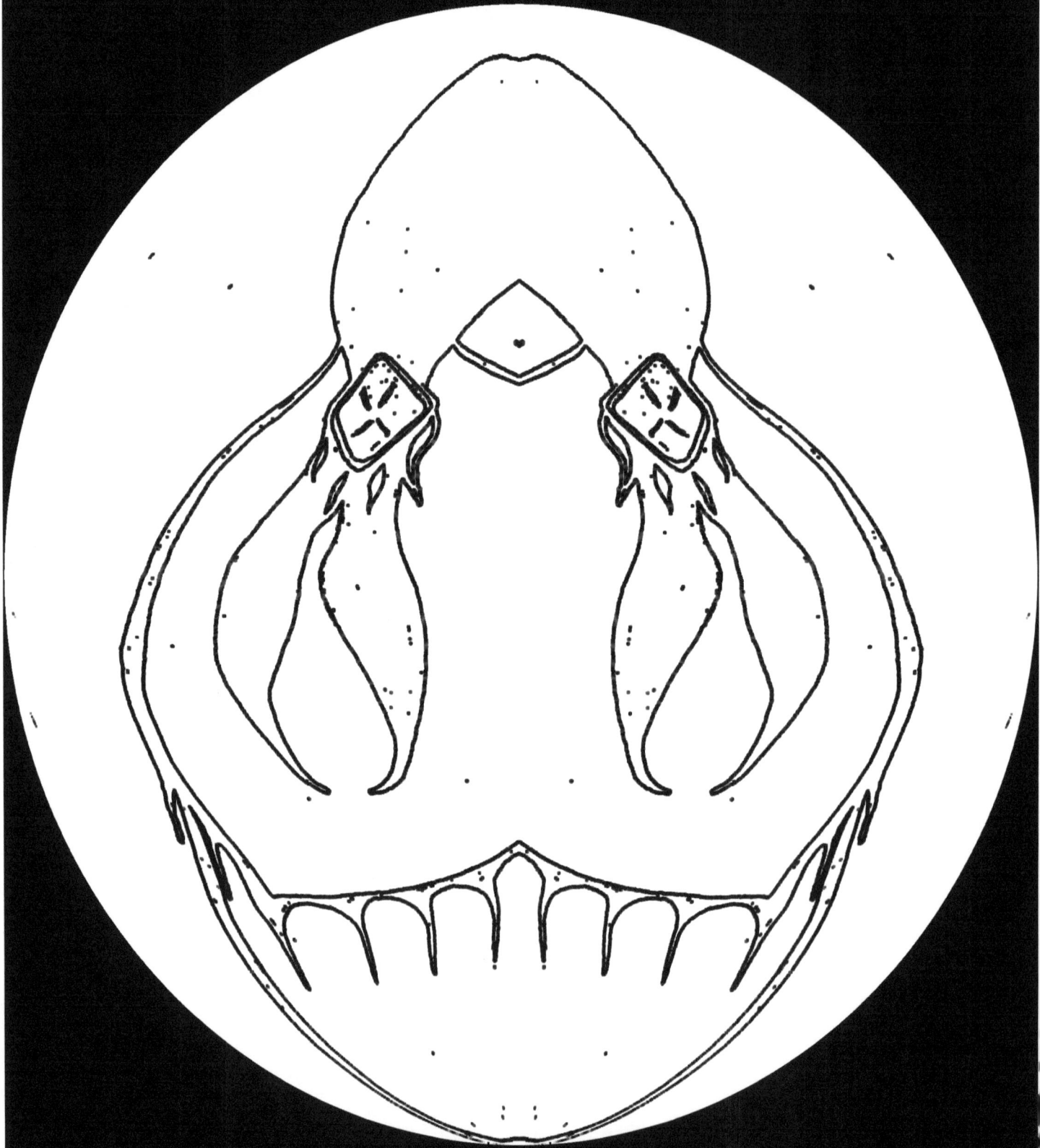

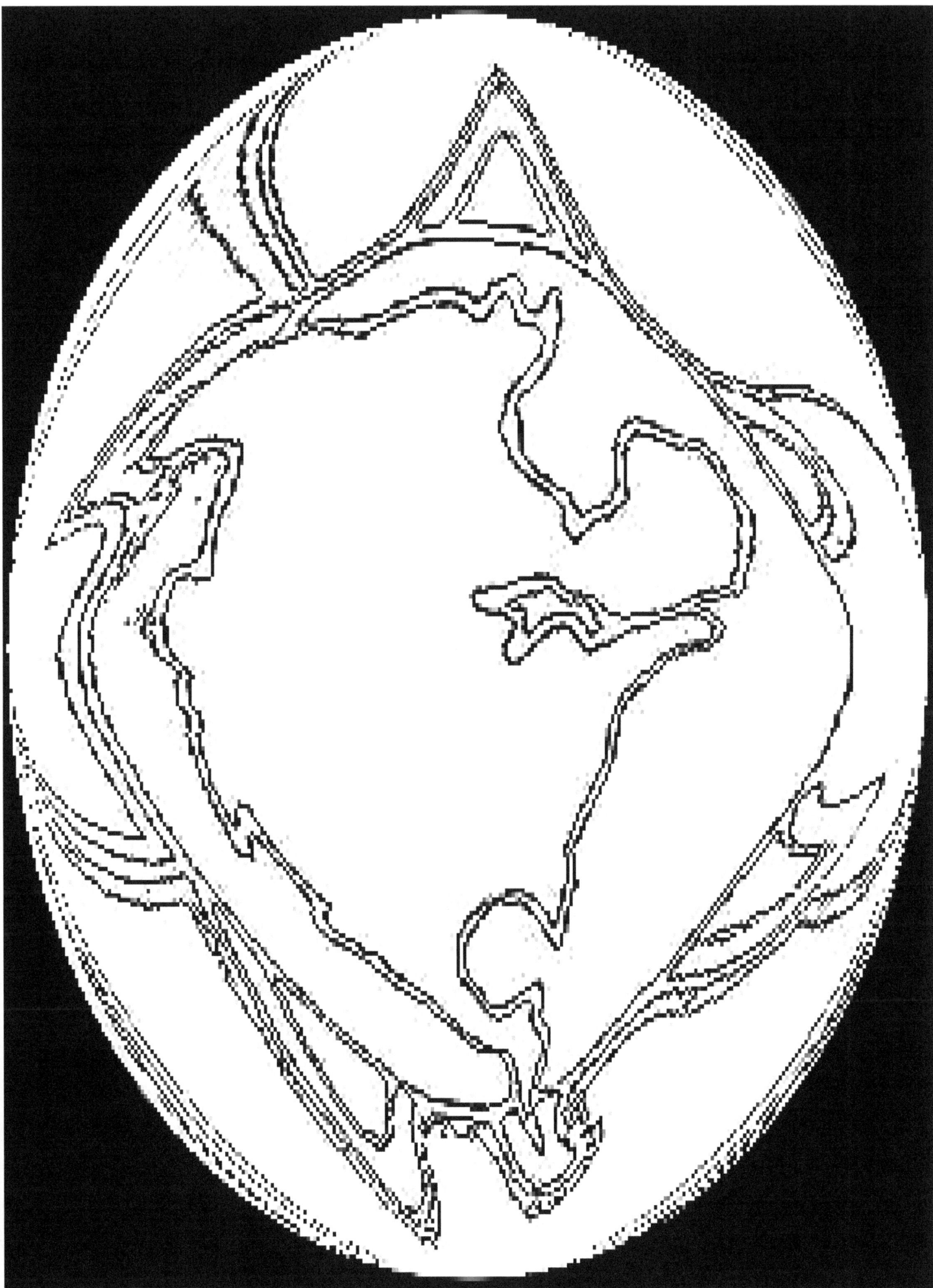

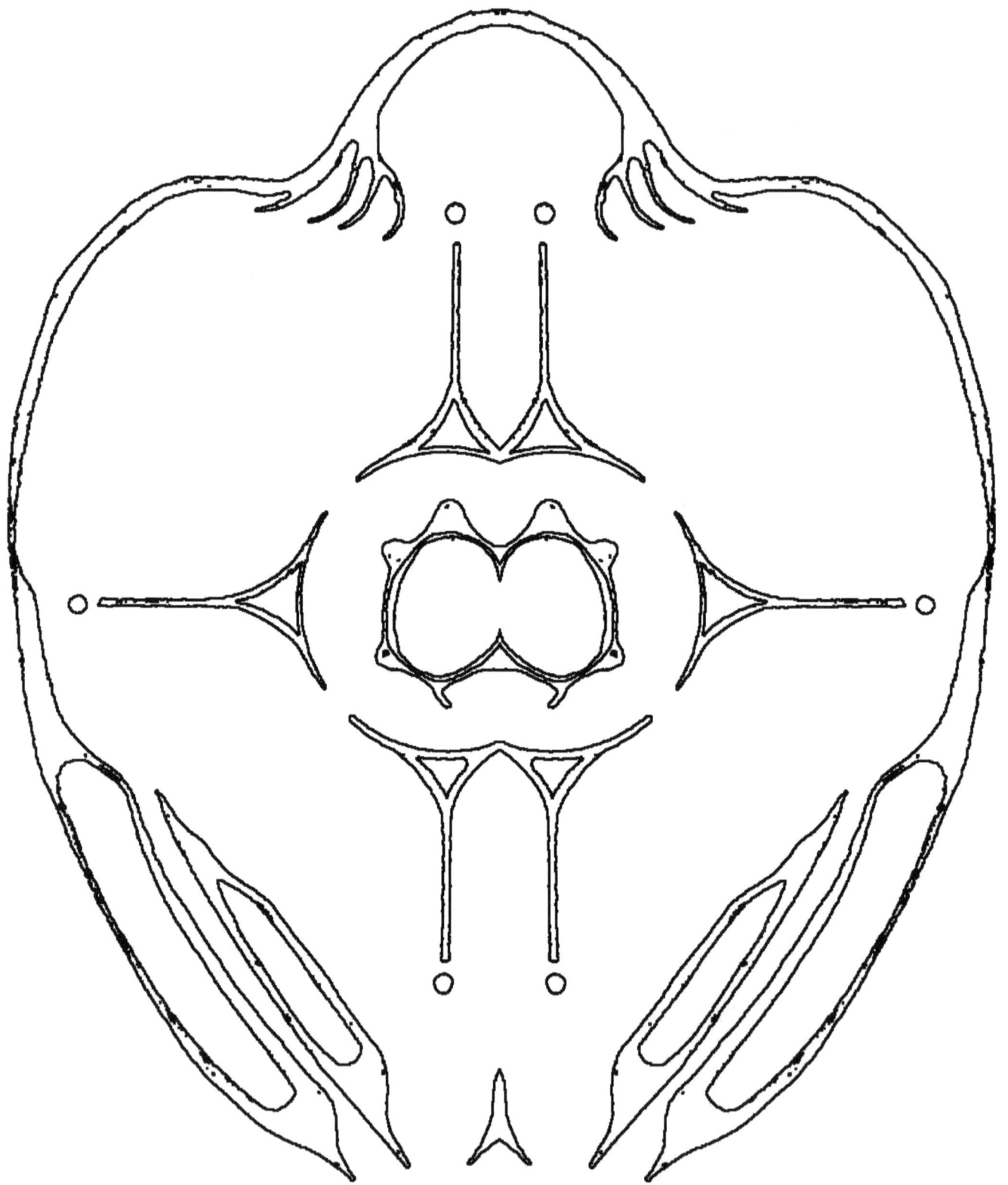

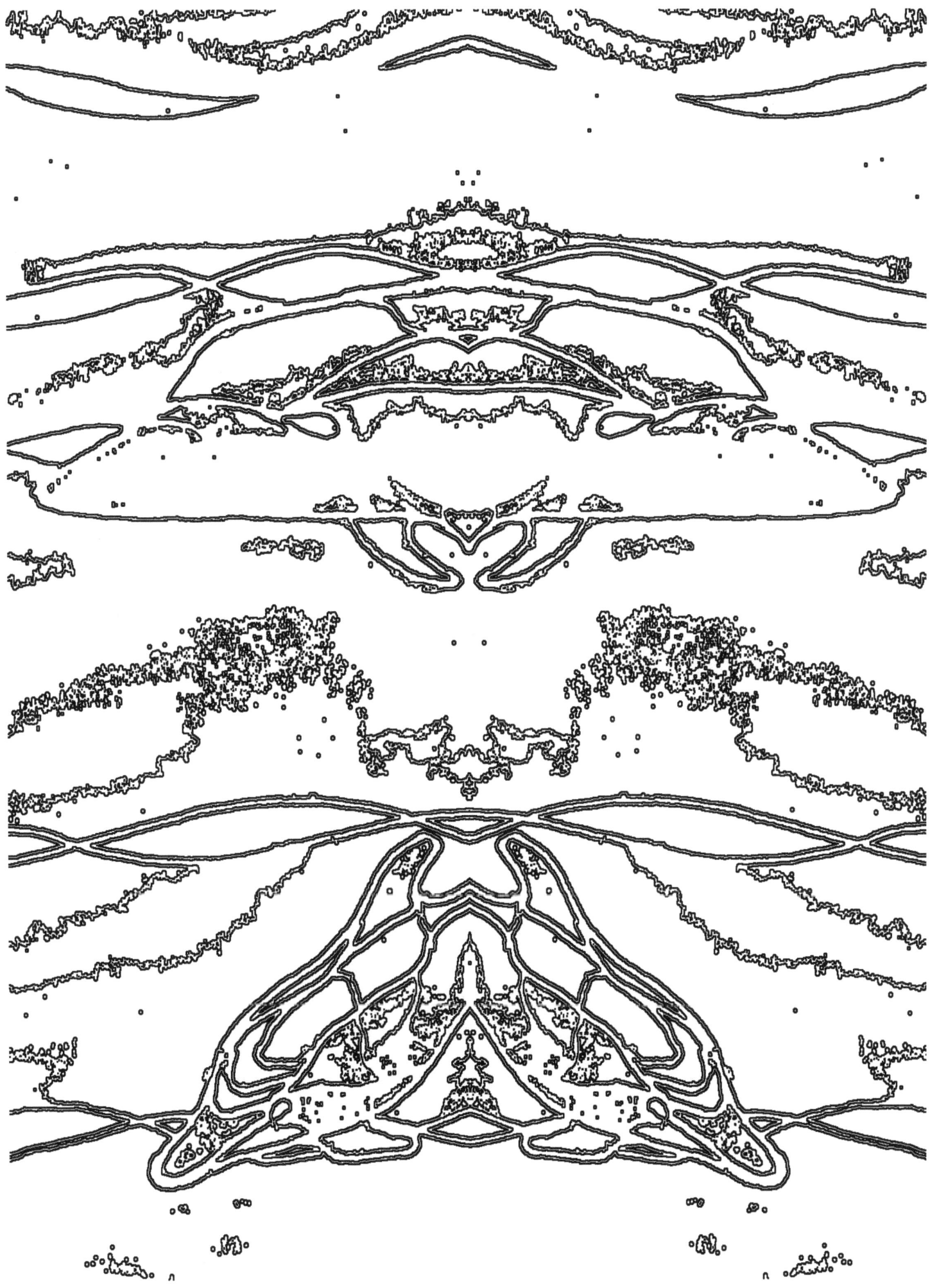

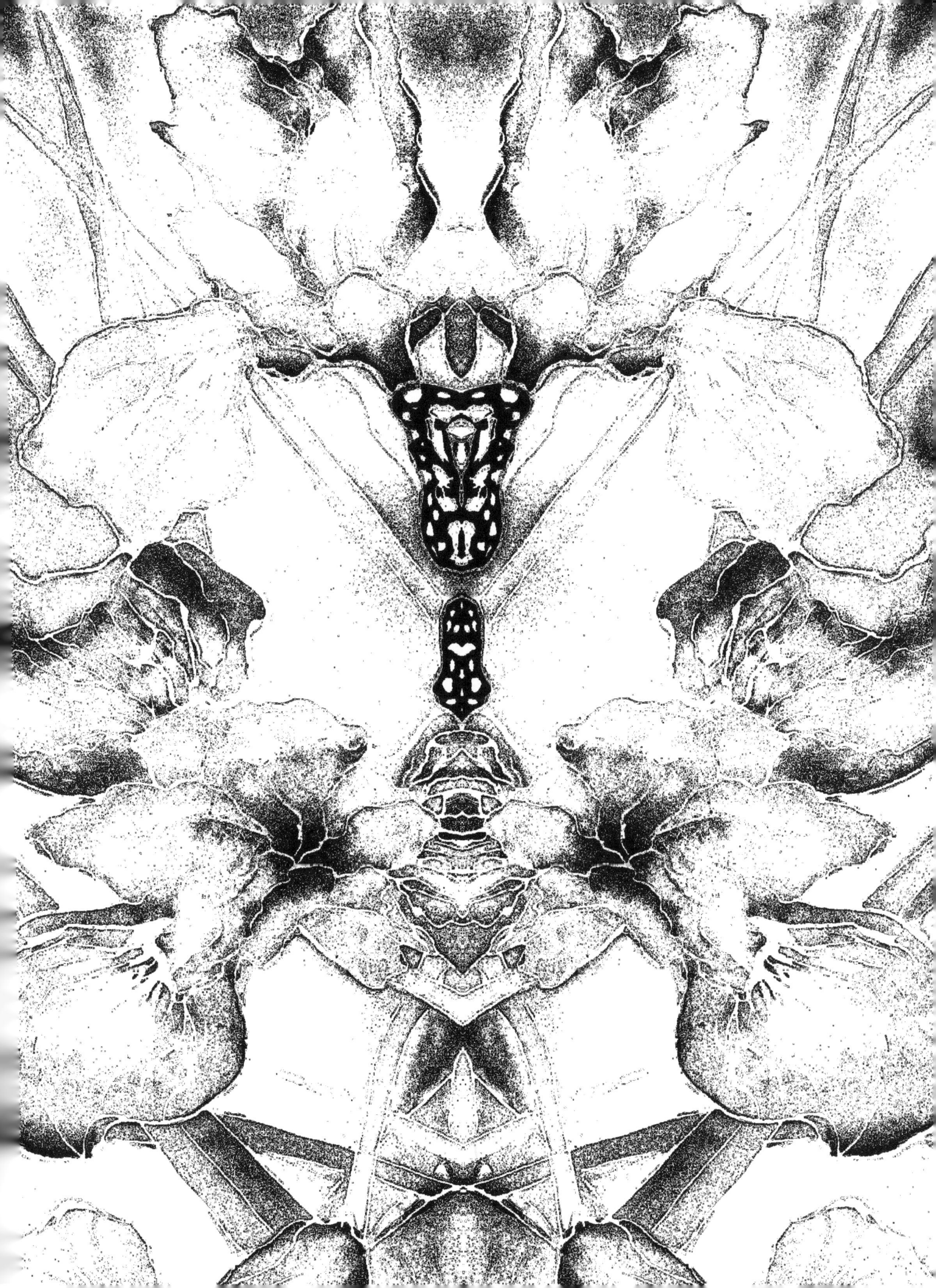

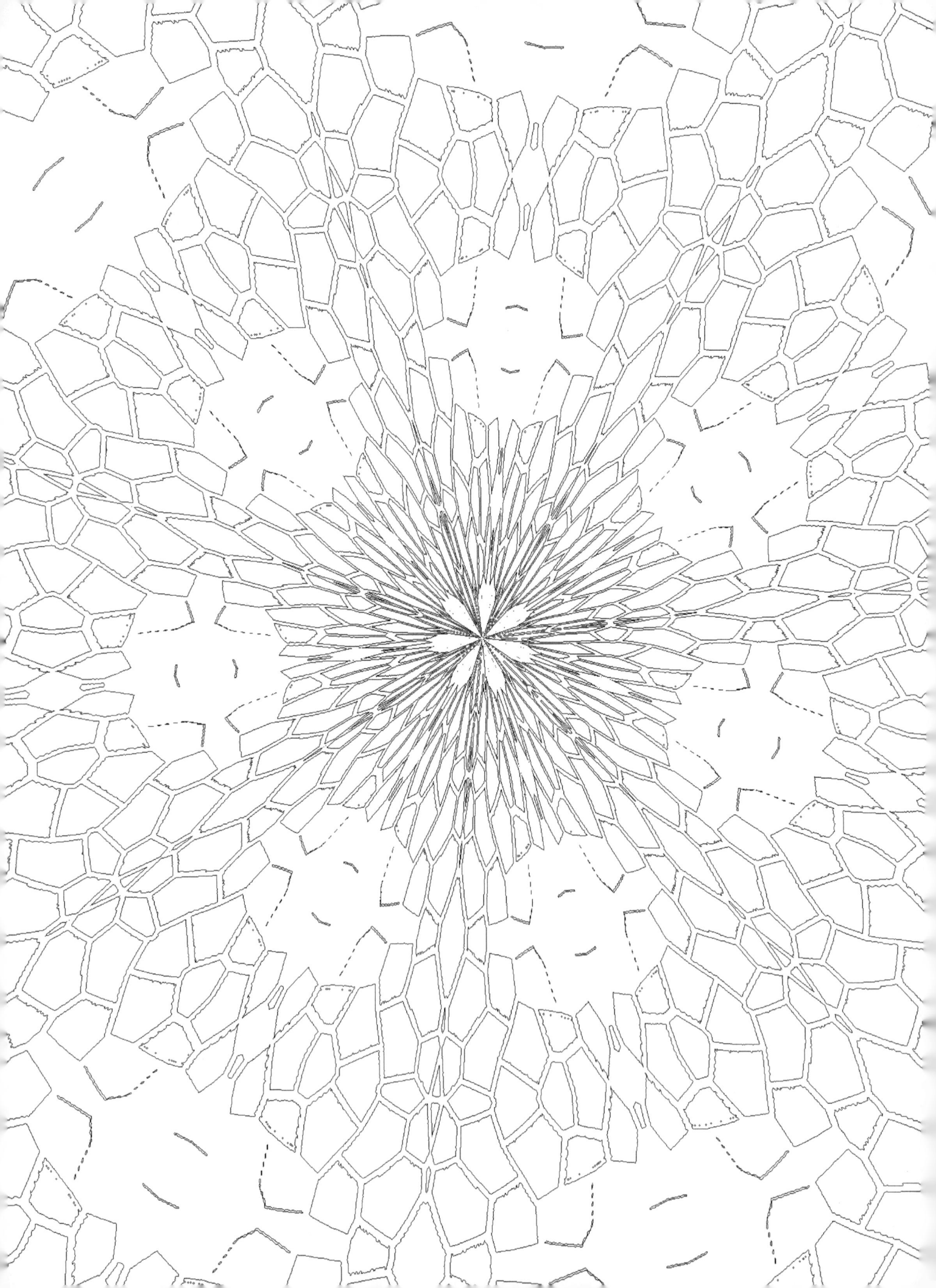

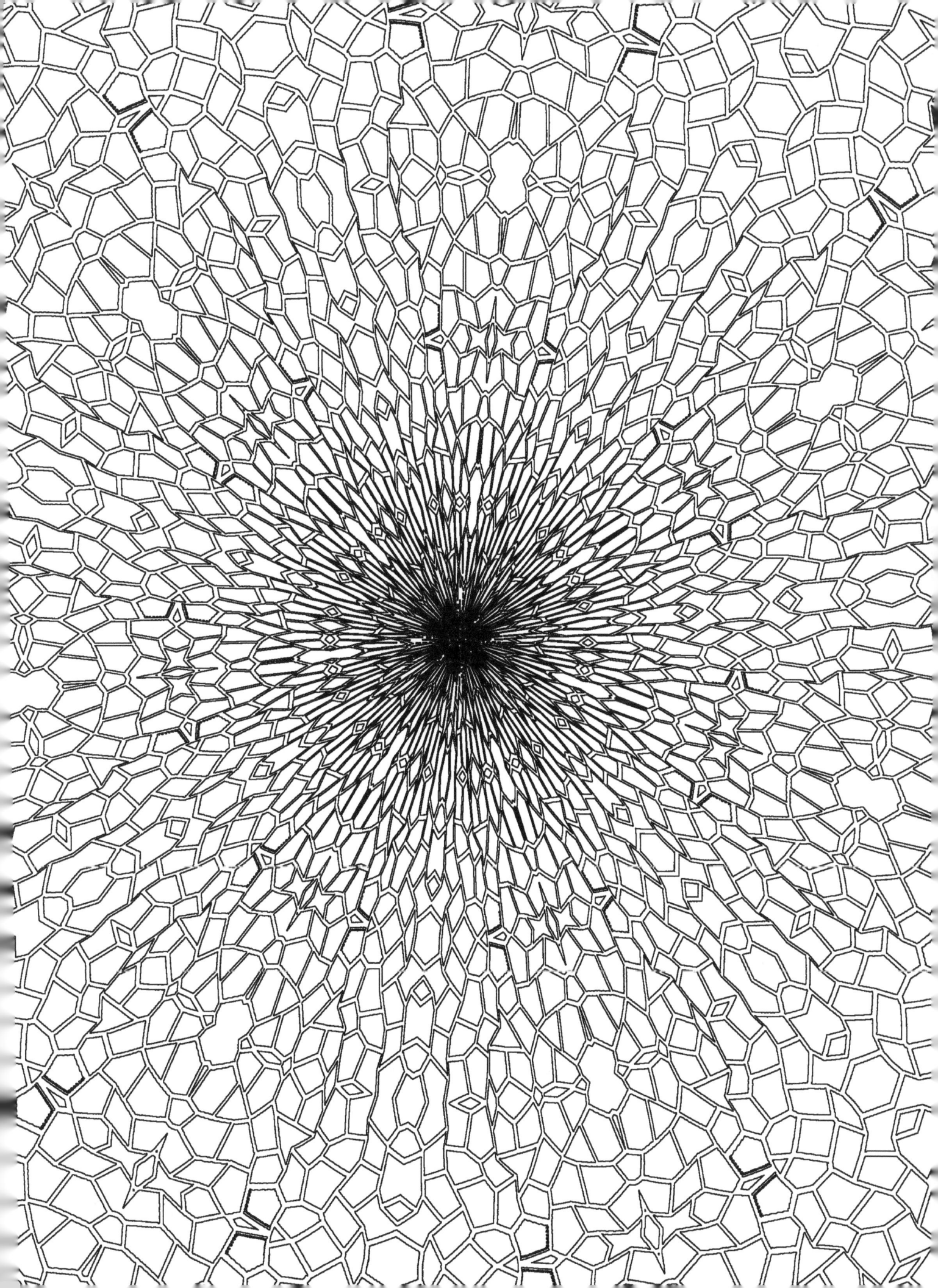

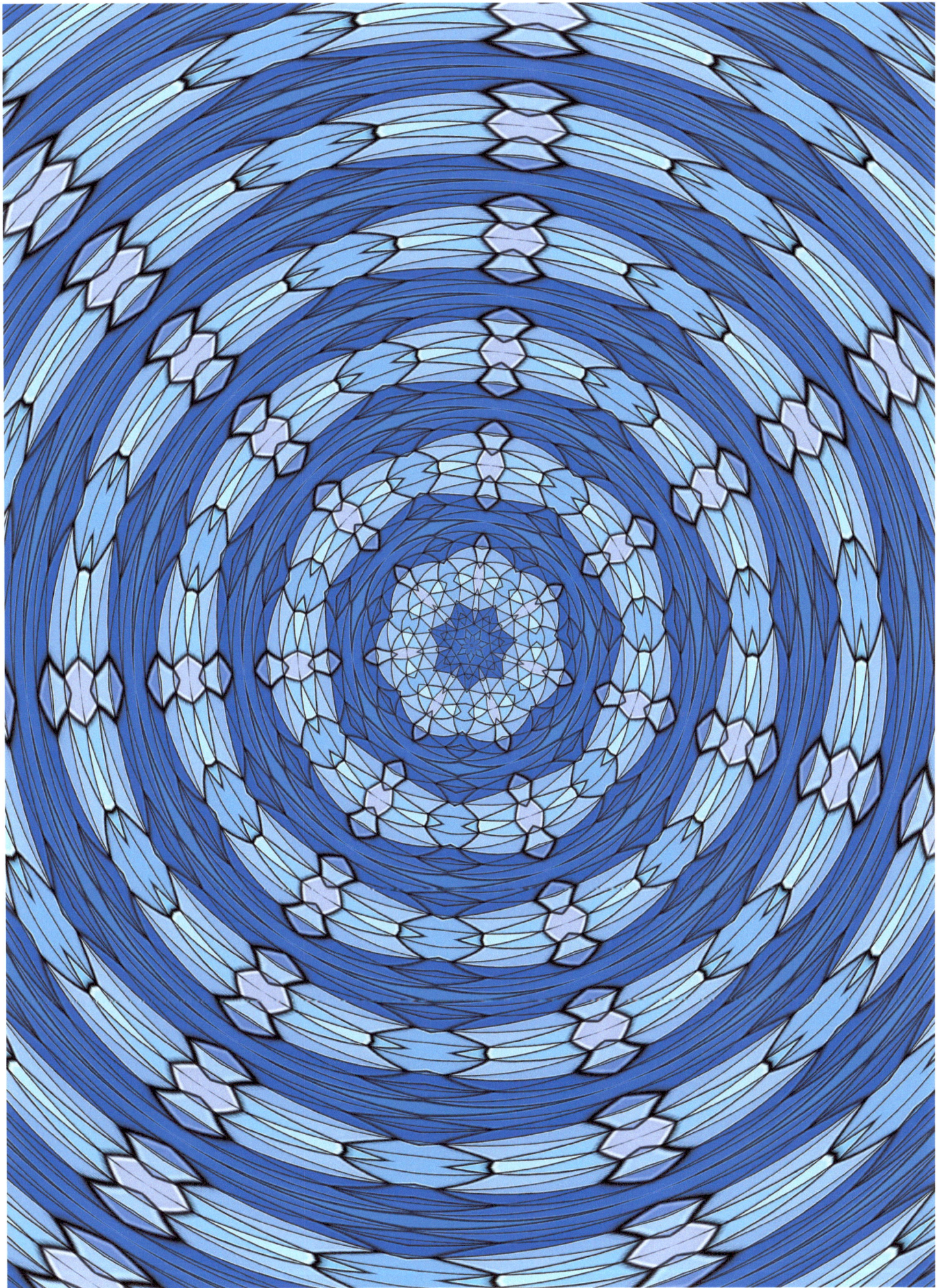

www.ingramcontent.com/pod-product-compliance
Lightning Source LLC
LaVergne TN
LVHW072100070426
835508LV00002B/190